Freedom
from Hurtful
Behaviors

What the Bible Teaches
about Liberation and Renewal

CHARLES T. KNIPPEL, PH.D.

CONCORDIA PUBLISHING HOUSE · SAINT LOUIS

*In Memory
of
My Parents,
Arthur and Lois Knippel,
and
My Grandmother,
Dorothy Knippel*

Contents

Preface

In recent years I have written two books that have to do with recovery from addictions. In the first, *The Twelve Steps: The Church's Challenge and Opportunity*, I discuss the origins and contents of the Twelve Step Spiritual Program of Recovery of Alcoholics Anonymous. This program has been adapted for use by many mutual-help groups. In addition, I evaluate the Steps from a biblical point of view and offer suggestions about how Christians can understand and respond to the Twelve Step Program.

In my second book, *When Addictions Threaten*, I provide information about both substance and behavior addictions and discuss resources available to Christians for preventing and recovering from addictions. The book offers practical help for individuals who are concerned about their addictions and those of people close to them.

Now I add a third book to supplement the two already published and to provide what they do not include. This third book sets forth in detail biblical truths intended to liberate us from the large number of persistent behaviors by which we disobey God and hurt ourselves and others. These truths are 12 in number and follow the format of A.A.'s Twelve Steps that I evaluated in my first book. However, the truths I formulate and discuss in this book are much different than A.A.'s Twelve Steps. A.A.'s Steps reflect facets of Bible teaching, but they are not explicitly Christian in content and therefore not fully biblical in their message. My book is different. It sets forth God's very own truths, revealed in the Bible, by which He provides the fullness of His blessings in Christ to liberate us from disobedient behaviors by which we hurt ourselves and others and to empower us for growth in Christian living.

God can and does help us find freedom from hurtful behaviors. In Christ, our lives can and do change. Like St. Paul, who said he often did not do the good he wanted to do (Romans 7:21), we Christians daily sin much. We will not be perfect in this world. Our Christian lives are always a struggle against sin. That struggle is empowered by God's forgiveness in Christ and His gift of the Holy Spirit. We have our successes and failures, our ups and downs. Still, God promises to help us in our daily struggles and give us successes. He promises to lift us up when we fall and to give us successes in the direction of Christian freedom and growth.

God faithfully keeps his promises to us. He liberates and renews us. With God's help many people are overcoming their hurtful behaviors. For example, by God's grace many are recovering from alcohol and drug addictions. We gratefully recall the words of St. Paul, "We were therefore buried with him [Christ] through Baptism into death in order that, just as Christ was raised from the dead through the glory of the Father, we too may live a new life" (Romans 6:4).

In this book, like the two preceding it, I make use of my doctoral research on the theological origins of A.A.'s Twelve Step Spiritual Program of Recovery. In addition, I draw on my theological and historical studies and my experience in the fields of pastoral ministry, addictions therapy, and seminary education.

Introduction

People from all walks of life yearn to be free from behaviors that hurt themselves and others. We want to live happy and productive lives. But by relying only on ourselves, we find that freedom is impossible to achieve. We find ourselves enslaved by injurious ways of behaving. These hurtful ways have to do with our inaccurate thoughts and beliefs, negative feelings, and wrong actions.

Through the years many have attempted to discover keys of liberation for persons enslaved by hurtful behaviors. Among these persons was Bill W., a cofounder of Alcoholics Anonymous. Under the tutelage of Samuel M. Shoemaker, an Episcopal priest associated with the Oxford Group Movement, he discovered principles that afforded him and others freedom from their enslavement to alcohol and launched them on a life of sobriety. On the basis of these principles he drafted a program of 12 steps, or 12 principles, which he called The Twelve Step Spiritual Program of Recovery. Since the 1930s these steps have afforded recovery for millions of alcoholics and others addicted to a variety of substances and behaviors. The steps generate a psychological or personality change sufficient to empower people to recover from addictions and attain improvement of their physical and emotional health.

Because the Twelve Steps were formulated to give aid and assistance to people of various beliefs and of no belief, they speak of God in generic terms—as "a Power greater than ourselves" and as "God *as we understood him.*" From a Christian perspective, the Twelve Steps are lacking and misleading.

By reestablishing these principles in the fullness of Bible teaching, we are able to possess tools for liberation and renewal that are truly from God and pleasing to God. They make available the benefits for wholeness that God the Father gives to people through the saving work of His Son, Jesus, and by the power of the Holy Spirit. They aid us in possessing a full share of the freedom, supplied by Jesus, that continually liberates and renews us at the very core of our being. All of this, of course, is because Jesus came to bring us freedom from our guilt, God's condemnation, and our enslavement to sin. This freedom from guilt and sin is ours because Jesus fulfilled God's Law perfectly, having lived without sin among us as a man. It is ours because He died on a cross to pay the penalty for our sins, and rose from the dead to be our victorious Lord.

With this perspective in mind, my purpose in this book is to provide biblical truths for liberation from hurtful behaviors and to present biblical resources and Christian suggestions for the implementation of each truth for newness of life. People of the Christian faith may use the truths and recommendations of this book in Christian mutual-help groups or use them privately to deal with self-identified harmful thoughts, emotions, and actions. Some may want to use this book to assist them in practicing the Twelve Step Program from a Christian perspective in a mutual-aid group to which they belong.

My hope is that this book, written in everyday language, will be useful to people in all walks of life who desire, or come to desire, freedom from hurtful ways of living and

to caregivers who are committed to helping people who suffer from a lack of freedom in the ways they think, feel, and
behave. All of us may most certainly claim the promise of
Jesus, "If you hold to My teaching, you are really My disciples. Then you will know the truth, and the truth will set
you free" (John 8:31–32).

1

The Variety
of Hurtful Behaviors

Hurtful Behaviors of the Mind

In this book I distinguish between mind behaviors (a person's processes of thought and feeling) and body behaviors (physical actions). I view the mind as that part of a person that thinks, reasons, believes, feels, wills, and perceives. I look upon the body as the physical part of a person that is organized for action. As does Scripture, I think of the human person as a unity having the aspects of body, mind, spirit, and soul.

The distinction that I make between mind and body does not intend to indicate that mind and body and their behaviors are not related. They are very much interrelated. Wrong beliefs, thoughts, and attitudes at work within the mind lead to painful emotions and hurtful actions.

In his letters St. Paul identifies a variety of hurtful behaviors of the mind. He mentions bitterness, anger, hatred, rage, malice, greed, impurity, envy, jealousy, and selfish ambition (Galatians 5:19–21; Ephesians 4:31; 5:3–6; 1 Corinthians 6:9–10).

We can readily relate to St. Paul's list of hurtful mind behaviors by including other attitudes and feelings associated with negative thinking or inaccurate beliefs. We might add depression, worry, arrogance, paranoia, snobbishness, resentment, suspiciousness, indifference, fear, shame, obstinacy, sadness, unrealistic guilt, and low self-esteem. This list, of course, is not complete.

Hurtful Behaviors of the Body

St. Paul speaks extensively about hurtful actions. A partial list of such body behaviors includes brawling, slander, sexual immorality, obscenity, foolish talk, coarse joking, fits of rage, drunkenness, swindling, thievery, idolatry, witchcraft, rioting, and factiousness (Galatians 5:19–21; Ephesians 4:31; 1 Corinthians 6:9–10). Today we might supplement St. Paul's list by adding the abuse of alcohol, drugs, food, work, money, power, and relationships.

Hurtful Behaviors Dishonor God and Harm Us and Others

Wrong beliefs, thoughts, attitudes, feelings, and actions dishonor God and hurt us and others. They dishonor God and injure us and others because such behaviors are counter to God's will for us. In the Ten Commandments God has shown us a way of living that is both obedient to Him and beneficial for us and others. When we disobey God we sin. We not only dishonor Him and incur His displeasure but, at the same time, inevitably hurt ourselves and others. When we speak of behaviors that hurt us and others, we are talking about sinful behaviors that disobey and dishonor God. These are the behaviors that harm us and others. For example, take King David. He dishonored and angered God and hurt himself and others when he had sexual desire for Bathsheba, the wife of Uriah, and had an adulterous affair with her. He ultimately had Bathsheba's husband killed in battle, so that he might have her as his wife.

11

Then there is the cowardice and denial of Peter. He thought he was in grave danger, feared Jesus' enemies, and denied Jesus. He sinned, and in pain and repentance he wept. In sadness and compassion Jesus looked on Peter. And there is the story of Judas. He loved money. As a result, he betrayed Jesus to Jewish religious leaders for 30 pieces of silver. This betrayal led to Jesus' crucifixion. Judas was filled with remorse and hanged himself. To the great sorrow of St. Paul, Demas, because he loved the world, deserted Paul and the Christian faith. God was dishonored by his apostasy, and Paul was deeply disappointed and hurt. Demas ruined his spiritual life and well-being.

I am sure we can all recall many times when we disobeyed and disrespected God and hurt ourselves and others because of beliefs, thoughts, attitudes, feelings, and actions that are contrary to God's will. We believe someone has criticized us unjustly. We feel angry, speak angry words, and break off our relationship with that person. We think someone has been more generous with another person than with us. We are jealous and begin saying bad things about the person we believe has disregarded us. We perceive that someone has kept us from getting a promotion at work. We feel resentment and do whatever we can to hurt that person's reputation. We imagine that we are inferior to other people; feel depressed, helpless, and inadequate; and drink excessively or abuse other drugs in an attempt to feel better about ourselves. In all of these instances we disobey and dishonor God and damage ourselves and others. God is disrespected, and we and those about us suffer severe pain.

Hurtful Behaviors Enslave

The Bible regards the hurtful mental and physical

behaviors of which we speak as sins. As such they are behaviors that have the power to enslave, for it is the nature of sin to enslave us. The writer to the Hebrews speaks of sin as a snare. He writes, "Let us throw off everything that hinders and the sin that so easily entangles" (Hebrews 12:1). As we persist in hurtful behaviors, we readily become obsessed with hurtful mental behaviors—our sinful thoughts, beliefs, attitudes, and feelings. We run them over and over in our minds. As we persist in behaviors, we easily become compulsively involved in them. We feel compelled to repeat them over and over. We discover ourselves losing control over both mental and physical behaviors. They begin to take possession of us and overpower us.

Repeated sins enslave us. Jesus observed this reality. He said, "Everyone who sins is a slave to sin" (John 8:34). St. Paul characterized sin as reigning in mortal bodies so that people obey its evil desires. He also spoke of sin's ability to master us (Romans 6:11–14). Paul wrote, "Don't you know that when you offer yourselves to someone to obey him as slaves, you are slaves to the one whom you obey—whether you are slaves to sin, which leads to death, or to obedience, which leads to righteousness?" (Romans 6:16).

St. Paul spoke of his own experience with sin as a Christian and at the same time described the experience of every Christian. In his Letter to the Romans he pointed out that as Christians we remain sinners even though our sins are forgiven and we daily are renewed by the Holy Spirit. Sin at work in us forcefully endeavors to take over our lives. We must be careful not to let sin control us. Paul wrote, "I find this law at work: When I want to do good, evil is right there with me. For in my inner being I delight in God's law; but I see another law at work in the members of my body, waging war against the law of my mind and making me a prisoner of the law of sin at work within my members" (Romans 7:21–23).

Freedom Is Needed

To escape the bondage of wrong beliefs, thoughts, feelings, and actions, as human beings we need to be liberated from our enslavement. Our greatest need is to be freed from all that disobeys God and thus harms us and others. We need to be freed from sin by God's intervention because we cannot free ourselves from our bondage. As God said through the apostle Paul, by nature we are worse than enslaved; we are "dead in [our] transgressions and sins" (Ephesians 2:1). In addition to being spiritually dead, we are spiritually blind and the enemies of God. These are the words of St. Paul: "The sinful mind is hostile to God" (Romans 8:7) and "The man without the Spirit does not accept the things that come from the Spirit of God, for they are foolishness to him, and he cannot understand them, because they are spiritually discerned" (1 Corinthians 2:14). Scripture makes clear that we do not have the ability to achieve a right relationship with God and to obtain His radically life-transforming power.

Also as Christians we need the liberating power of God to overcome the ever-present determination of our sinful nature to make us slaves once again to the power of sin. We cry out for freedom as did St. Paul: "What a wretched man I am! Who will rescue me from this body of death?" (Romans 7:24). As we shall discuss at length in pages to come, we can happily exclaim with St. Paul, "Thanks be to God—through Jesus Christ our Lord!" (Romans 7:25). God frees us from sin through Jesus Christ. We recall the words of Jesus, "If the Son sets you free, you will be free indeed" (John 8:36).

2

Liberating Truths
for Hurtful Behaviors

Bill W.'s Steps to Liberate Alcoholics

The truths of liberation for hurtful mental and physical behaviors that I discuss in this book follow the format of the Twelve Steps crafted by William Griffith Wilson (known in his anonymity as Bill W.) in consultation with other recovering alcoholics. He drafted them to liberate persons addicted to alcohol and to provide them with a sober lifestyle.

Wilson, a seriously ill alcoholic, found sobriety through his association with the Oxford Group Movement and especially with Dr. Samuel M. Shoemaker, an Episcopal priest and the American leader of the Oxford Groups for many years. He achieved sobriety in the mid 1930s by practicing the principles of the Oxford Groups, and he spoke of them as keys for liberation. At the time of Shoemaker's death, Wilson wrote:

> From his [Shoemaker's] teaching, Dr. Bob [a cofounder of A.A. together with Bill W.] and I absorbed most of the principles that were later embodied in the Twelve Steps of A.A. Our ideas of self-examination, acknowledgment of character defects, restitution for harm done and working with others come straight from Sam. Therefore he gave to us the concrete knowledge

of what we could do about our illness; he passed to us the spiritual keys by which so many of us have been liberated.[1]

Drawing on what Bill W. and his colleagues learned from Sam Shoemaker's Oxford Group, the new fellowship of recovering alcoholics had a word-of-mouth program the group summarized in six steps as follows:

1. We admitted that we were licked, that we were powerless over alcohol.

2. We made an inventory of our defects or sins.

3. We confessed or shared our shortcomings with another person in confidence.

4. We made restitution to all those we had harmed by our drinking.

5. We tried to help other alcoholics, with no thought of reward in money or prestige.

6. We prayed to whatever God we thought there was for power to practice these precepts.[2]

On the basis of these steps Bill W., in consultation with Dr. Bob and other recovering alcoholics, drafted the Twelve Step Spiritual Program of Recovery, first published in the book *Alcoholics Anonymous* in 1939. Bill wrote:

Remember that we deal with alcohol—cunning, baffling, powerful! Without help it is too much for us. But there is One who has all power—that One is God. May you find Him now!

Half measures availed us nothing. We stood at the turning point. We asked His protection and care with complete abandon.

Here are the steps we took, which are suggested as a Program of Recovery.

1. We admitted we were powerless over alcohol—that our lives had become unmanageable.

2. Came to believe that a Power greater than ourselves could restore us to sanity.

3. Made a decision to turn our will and our lives over to the care of God *as we understood Him.*

4. Made a searching and fearless moral inventory of ourselves.

5. Admitted to God, to ourselves, and to another human being the exact nature of our wrongs.

6. Were entirely ready to have God remove all these defects of character.

7. Humbly asked Him to remove our shortcomings.

8. Made a list of all persons we had harmed, and became willing to make amends to them all.

9. Made direct amends to such people wherever possible, except when to do so would injure them or others.

10. Continued to take personal inventory and when we were wrong promptly admitted it.

11. Sought through prayer and meditation to improve our conscious contact with God *as we understood Him,* praying only for knowledge of His will for us and the power to carry that out.

12. Having had a spiritual awakening as the result of these steps, we tried to carry this message to alcoholics, and to practice these principles in all our affairs.[3]

Since 1939 many mutual-help groups have come to make use of A.A.'s Twelve Steps, usually with only a minor change to Steps 1 and 12 that originally applied the steps only to the abuse of alcohol and to alcoholics. Among such mutual-help groups are Al-Anon, Narcotics Anonymous, Gamblers Anonymous, Overeaters Anonymous, Smokers Anonymous, Sexaholics Anonymous, and Codependents Anonymous. Millions of people are recovering from their hurtful behaviors by practicing the Twelve Step Program.

The Necessity for Christian Truths

Even though the Oxford Groups took many of their teachings from the Bible, and Bill W. built on those teachings, the Twelve Steps are not explicitly Christian in their content. As a matter of fact, basic Christian teachings were omitted so that the Steps might be acceptable to people of many faiths or of no faith at all. Thus there is no mention of Jesus, and God is defined as "as Power greater than ourselves" and as "God as we understood Him." Furthermore, even though the Steps produce for many, by the goodness of God, a personality change sufficient to bring about recovery from alcoholism, the Steps wrongly suggest that the doing of the Steps produces or enhances a saving relationship with God. In contrast the Bible teaches that God is the triune God—one God in three persons: Father, Son, and Holy Spirit. According to the Bible, we obtain a right relationship with God only through faith in Jesus Christ as our Savior from the guilt, power, and consequences of sin.

Since, however, Bill W.'s Steps have their roots in teachings of the Bible, we can use them to aid us in formulating and practicing ways of liberation and renewal that are faithfully rooted in the whole counsel of God revealed to us in Holy Scripture. We are blessed to possess and practice truths that are Christ-centered.

Biblical Truths for Liberation and Renewal

The biblical truths for freedom from hurtful behaviors and renewal of life, which we will discuss in detail in forthcoming chapters, are those I now propose.[4] Beginning with a prefatory statement, they read as follows:

God has called us to be His own in Jesus Christ. He has given us the gift of repentance to acknowledge our sins and to trust in Jesus Christ for the forgiveness of sins and the newness of life. Because God has made us His forgiven and renewed people, we are able to [do the steps that follow]:

1. Recognize and admit that we continue to be sinners even though we are restored to God's presence and power through the forgiveness of sins that we obtain through faith in Jesus Christ. We acknowledge that we daily sin much and are powerless over aspects of our thinking, feeling, and doing that are not yet under the influence of the Holy Spirit and thus produce sinful behaviors by which we disobey and dishonor God and hurt ourselves and others.

2. Believe that the God of our salvation daily forgives our sins for the sake of Jesus and, in our struggle with sin, renews us through the working of the Holy Spirit first received in Holy Baptism.

3. Live each day under the Holy Spirit's power so that, in the promise and new life of Holy Baptism, we decisively turn our wills and our lives over to the care of God and His re-creating power and make fuller use of His gift of the Holy Spirit to obtain freedom from our controlling sinful behaviors of mind and body.

4. Make a searching and fearless inventory of our besetting sinful and hurtful behaviors of mind and

19

body that require immediate attention.

5. Acknowledge to ourselves and confess to God and another Christian the exact nature of our sinful and hurtful behaviors. Mindful of the comforting and reassuring benefits of individual absolution, we value the opportunity to make private confession before the pastor and receive individual absolution from God through him as God's representative.

6. Be ready and willing to have God remove our sinful and hurtful behaviors of mind and body.

7. Ask God, with a humble mind, to remove our sinful and hurtful thoughts, emotions, and actions.

8. Make a list of all persons we have harmed and be willing to make amends to each of them.

9. Make direct amends to the people we have hurt when it is possible to do so without hurting them or others.

10. Continue day by day to take a personal inventory and when we sin, promptly acknowledge and confess our sins, ask God's forgiveness for Jesus' sake, and receive God's forgiveness and liberating power to find freedom from disobedient and hurtful behaviors.

11. Use the Word of God and the Lord's Supper to enhance our faith relationship with God, and through the use of God's Word and prayer obtain a clearer understanding of God's will that the Holy Spirit empowers us to carry out.

12. Pass on the saving and liberating Good News of Jesus Christ to all in need of God's love and power to overcome sinful and hurtful behaviors, and seek to live every facet of our lives in the freedom of God's people.

Benefits of Biblical Truths

What are the benefits of the biblical truths of liberation? What do they offer that other things, such as the Twelve Steps, do not offer? First of all, the biblical truths insure that we are looking for help where the full and powerful help we need is to be found. They assure us that we are depending on the true and living God, whom Scripture declares to be the only God. He is the one Divine Being who has revealed Himself in Scripture as Father, Son, and Holy Spirit. He is the God of our creation and salvation. We do not have to wonder who God is or how to understand Him. He makes Himself known to us.

Second, the God on whom we depend in applying Christian truths assures us beyond any doubt that in Christ we do indeed have a right relationship with Him and authentically possess the forgiveness of sins. We do not simply wish for God's love and forgiveness. We do not suppose that we may obtain a right relationship with God by simply wanting it or because of some actions of our own. We are fully assured of God's love because of the life and death and resurrection Jesus Christ. We believe what Scripture teaches—that Jesus died and rose from the dead to pay the debt for our sinfulness and sin and to free us from the guilt, punishment, and power of sin. We know with certainty and confidence that we are restored to God's presence and power through faith in Jesus Christ as the Savior and Lord of our lives. We do not have to wonder if God loves us or simply wish that God may love and accept us. We can and do confidently believe we live in God's love because it is His sure and certain gift, the blessing of His undeserved favor in Christ.

In the third place, God's love for us in Christ has an effect on our behavior. We have the life-transforming power of God Himself available to us. When God forgives us our sins for Jesus' sake and claims us as His own, He gives us the gift of His Holy Spirit, who renews our lives. Zacchaeus quit cheating people. Unstable Peter became a powerful preacher. Saul the blasphemer was transformed into the apostle Paul, who later said, "We are God's workmanship, created in Christ Jesus to do good works" (Ephesians 2:10) and "Do not let sin reign in your mortal body" (Romans 6:12). It is the Holy Spirit who enables us to find in God's Law not only condemnation but guidance.

The use of biblical liberating truths produces more than a psychological change. It produces God-generated radical changes in our mental and physical behaviors because God Himself works through His Word at the center of our lives as spiritual beings. He sets us free from all that hurts us and others. By His own presence and power in our lives God enables us both to will and to do of His good pleasure. St. Paul affirms, "It is God who works in you to will and to act according to His good purpose" (Philippians 2:13).

3

Assumptions of Biblical Truths for Liberation and Renewal

The biblical assumptions for the Christian truths are summarized thus: "God has called us to be His own in Jesus Christ. He has given us the gift of repentance to acknowledge our sins and to trust in Jesus Christ for the forgiveness of sins and the newness of life. Because God has made us His forgiven and renewed people, we are able to [do the steps that follow]."

Only Christians can apply the biblical truths of liberation. We do not become Christians by carrying out Christian truths. Practicing Christian liberating truths does not in any way make us a Christian. We practice them and can practice them, even if imperfectly on this side of heaven, only because we *are* Christians.

The 12 Christian truths are for those endowed with repentance by God Himself. God's gift of repentance means that God has given us a new mind. Through His Word of Law He has shown us our sins and their dire consequences. Through His Gospel He has told us about the good news of Jesus Christ. He has given us faith to trust in Jesus Christ for the forgiveness of sins. He has given us a new life that seeks to obey God and do good both for self and others. Through faith God frees us from the guilt, condemnation, and bondage of sin. Thus by the power of the Holy Spirit we are able to live toward doing what Christian liberating truths instruct us to do. We are able to put our freedom into action. We may sometimes falter, even fail, but we press on toward greater freedom empowered by God's forgiving love and His energizing Spirit.

Truly God is good, gracious, and merciful to us. He does not hold our sins against us; He forgives our sins. But also, in His great goodness, He does not leave us in the misery of living sin-enslaved lives. He does not allow us to continue to live lives destructively enslaved by disobedient and hurtful behaviors. He transforms our lives. He re-creates us by His Holy Spirit for His glory, for our great benefit, and for the well-being of others. He gives us lives worth living, lives filled with the fruit of the Spirit—"love, joy, peace, patience, kindness, goodness, faithfulness, gentleness and self-control" (Galatians 5:22). "If anyone is in Christ, he is a new creation; the old has gone, the new has come! All this is from God, who reconciled us to Himself through Christ. . . . God made Him who had no sin to be sin for us, so that in Him we might become the righteousness of God" (2 Corinthians 5:17–18, 21). Thanks be to God!

Let us be clear: That we are forgiven and renewed does not mean that we are perfect. As Christians we are at the same time saints and sinners. Even though we are people of faith and new life, there are still parts of our thinking, feeling, and doing that are not under the influence of the Holy Spirit. We continue daily to sin much. Sin stands at the door of our lives, eager to enslave us and destroy our faith.

The insidious efforts of sin mean that each day we must by grace make deliberate and energetic use of the good influences of the Holy Spirit at work in us as Christians to turn to Jesus for pardon for our sins and to do what is good and right. Only the Gospel of His forgiveness keeps us in a right relationship with God, assures us of the Father's love, and provides us with a larger measure of His life-transforming power that renews our thoughts, shapes our feelings, and determines our actions. In other words, God calls us to practice daily the repentance He has given us in Holy Baptism and enables us to do so day by day. He empowers us to apply Christian truths in our lives. God frees us from harmful behaviors and renews our lives. He empowers us daily for awesome successes until in heaven He completely frees us from every sin and evil and perfectly transforms us.

In reviewing the assumptions of biblical truths for liberation and renewal, it is of greatest importance for us to remember and reaffirm emphatically that the life of freedom that God gives us on an ongoing basis is possible, and only possible, because of all Jesus Christ is and has done for us.

The Bible clearly teaches that Jesus Christ is the Son of God who, at a particular time in human history, became a human being by being born of the Virgin Mary. He came to put us in a right relationship with God through the forgiveness of sin. As the God-man, Jesus was completely obedient to God as He lived out the years of His life on earth. Yet, even though He was innocent of all wrongdoing, He was put to death by crucifixion. How does Scripture explain this? Scripture tells us that Jesus' suffering and death were in our stead and for our benefit. He allowed sinful and wicked people to put Him to death so that His suffering and death might satisfy God's wrath for every person's sin and disobedience. Jesus paid our debt before God. He traded places with us, and His death made good for our sinfulness and sin. Then, following His death, Jesus rose from the dead. His resurrection fully affirmed that the Father was pleased with His Son and accepted His death as a full payment for our rebellion again Him. "[Christ] was delivered over to death for our sins and was raised to life for our justification" (Romans 4:25).

The Scriptures are clear about the meaning of Jesus' death for all of us and everyone. The writer to the Hebrews proclaims:

> In the past God spoke to our forefathers through the prophets at many times and in various ways, but in these last days He has spoken to us by His Son, whom He appointed heir of all things, and through whom He made the universe. The Son is the radiance of God's glory and the exact representation of His being, sustaining all things by His powerful word. After He had provided purification for sins, He sat down at the right hand of the Majesty in heaven. (Hebrews 1:1–3)

St. Paul clearly states of Jesus, "God made Him who had no sin to be sin for us, so that in Him we might become the righteousness of God" (2 Corinthians 5:21). He also wrote, "For what I received I passed on to you as of first importance: that Christ died for our sins according to the Scriptures, that He was buried, that He was raised on the third day according to the Scriptures" (1 Corinthians 15:3–4). "Christ died for the ungodly. . . . God demonstrates His own love for us in this: While we were still sinners, Christ died for us" (Romans 5:6, 8). In the words of St. John, "He [Jesus] is the atoning sacrifice for our sins, and not only for ours but also for the sins of the whole world" (1 John 2:2).

What Jesus gained for us, the Father gives us through the Gospel as a gift of His grace (undeserved favor). We do not deserve God's love, earn it, or merit it. He forgives our sins and declares us righteous before Him when, by His gift of faith, we trust Jesus as the Savior the Father sent and depend on Him for pardon. In turn, God, who graciously accepts us as His own for Jesus' sake, gives us His Holy Spirit to transform our lives. In this way, and in this way only, God sets us free from the guilt, the curse, and the power of our sin. St. Paul writes, "By grace you have been saved, through faith—and this not from yourselves, it is the gift of God—not by works, so that no one can boast" (Ephesians 2:8–9). "Since we have been justified [declared just before God] through faith, we have peace with God through our Lord Jesus Christ, through whom we have gained access by faith into this grace in which we now stand" (Romans 5:1–2).

The Bible speaks of the liberation God gives as redemption. This means that Jesus paid the price to set us free from our captors. As Jesus Himself said, He gave His life as a ransom for us (Matthew 20:28). St. Peter says it this way, "For you know that it was not with perishable things such as silver or gold that you were redeemed from the empty way of life handed down to you from your forefathers, but with the precious blood of Christ, a lamb without blemish or defect" (1 Peter 1:18–19). In his Letter to the Galatians St. Paul writes:

> When we were children, we were in slavery under the basic principles of the world. But when the time had fully come, God sent His Son, born of a woman, born under law, to redeem those under law, that we might receive the full rights of sons. Because you are sons, God sent the Spirit of His Son into our hearts, the Spirit who calls out, "*Abba*, Father." So you are no longer a slave, but a son; and since you are a son, God has made you also an heir. (Galatians 4:3–7)

27

We also have Paul's words to the Colossians: "He [God] has rescued us from the dominion of darkness and brought us into the kingdom of the Son He loves, in whom we have redemption, the forgiveness of sins" (Colossians 1:13–14).

Jesus sums up what the Bible teaches: "I tell you the truth, everyone who sins is a slave to sin. Now a slave has no permanent place in the family, but a son belongs to it forever. So if the Son sets you free, you will be free indeed" (John 8:34–36).

4

Liberating Truths 1–3
Counting on God, Not Ourselves

Truth 1: Admission of Powerlessness

The first truth calls us to "recognize and admit that we continue to be sinners even though we are restored to God's presence and power through the forgiveness of sins that we obtain through faith in Jesus Christ. We acknowledge that we daily sin much and are powerless over aspects of our thinking, feeling, and doing that are not yet under the influence of the Holy Spirit and thus produce sinful behaviors by which we disobey and dishonor God and hurt ourselves and others."

We are applying liberating truths to our behaviors that persistently hurt us and others. It sounds easy to "recognize and admit that we continue to be sinners even though we are restored to God's presence and power through the forgiveness of sins that we obtain through faith in Jesus Christ" and "that we daily sin much and are powerless over aspects of our thinking, feeling, and doing that are not yet under the influence of the Holy Spirit." But in reality it is not always as easy as it may sound. Even though we are Christians, we often minimize sin in our lives. We downplay its seriousness.

Not only do we minimize, but even more seriously, we frequently deny to ourselves and to others that we daily sin much, especially that we "are powerless over aspects of our thinking, feeling, and doing that are not yet under the influence of the Holy Spirit" and that these facets of our lives are reason for grave concern. This is the kind of denial that usually accompanies hurtful obsessive thoughts, persistent negative feelings, and compulsive destructive behaviors. We become slaves to our behaviors and to our denial of them. We suffer loss of control over the ways we think, feel, and act. In A.A., persons introduce themselves by saying, "My name is _____ and I'm an alcoholic" or "My name is _____ and I'm a recovering alcoholic." In this way they acknowledge that they are powerless over alcohol and that recovery is possible only by admitting that they have lost control over their use of alcohol. This admission, overcoming denial, is essential to recovery.

Denied hurtful mental and physical behaviors seriously jeopardize our spiritual well-being. They are enslaving behaviors that threaten our faith relationship with God. They may not immediately destroy our faith when they are born of weakness and perpetuated by our loss of control over them. Even weak faith is saving faith because faith is the Holy Spirit's gift to us. But ultimately unrepented sins of weakness erode and destroy our faith. They thrust God and His life out of our lives.

We desperately need to recognize our powerlessness over facets of our lives that are not under the control of the Holy Spirit. What might some of these facets be? First, our powerlessness over erroneous and unrelenting thoughts or beliefs about ourselves and/or others: "I'm not a good person"; "I never do anything right"; "No one likes me"; "People are always trying to hurt me"; "No one appreciates me"; "The future looks hopeless"; "I don't matter to God." Second, our powerlessness over persistent and painful feelings: unrealistic guilt, worthlessness, sadness, jealousy, resentment, hatred, fear, shame, disappointment, and loneliness. Third, our powerlessness over recurrent injurious behaviors: overeating, abusive and alcoholic drinking, drug abuse, gambling, wrong sexual activity, excessive Internet use, overspending, workaholism, controlling activities, stealing, gossiping, slander, use of profanity, lying, physical abuse, depreciating and disrespectful language.

All too frequently we and others fall prey to the behaviors we have mentioned and to many others that are equally detrimental. But because we tend to deny, minimize, and rationalize our bad behaviors, in order to change we usually need to suffer severe and undeniable pain from the wrong ways we function mentally and physically—pain that outweighs whatever benefits we suppose we receive from behaving as we do. In the depths of pain, and only then, we begin to recognize the frightening reality of our faltering condition and our utter and complete powerlessness to liberate ourselves. Then we are able to share St. Paul's experience much more painfully and beneficially and cry out for help. St. Paul exclaimed:

> I know that nothing good lives in me, that is, in my sinful nature. For I have the desire to do what is good, but I cannot carry it out. For what I do is not the good I want to do; no, the evil I do not want to do—this I keep on doing. . . . What a wretched man I am! Who will rescue me from this body of death? Thanks be to God—through Jesus Christ our Lord! (Romans 7:18–19, 24)

31

Before Jesus Christ can help us, we must admit our complete powerlessness to help ourselves. Showing great insight, Bill W. observed, "We shall find no enduring strength until we first admit complete defeat."[1] He spoke of the admission of powerlessness as the "bedrock upon which happy and purposeful lives may be built."[2]

Truth 2: Trust in God for Help

The second truth summons us to "believe that the God of our salvation daily forgives our sins for the sake of Jesus, and, in our struggle with sin, renews us through the working of the Holy Spirit first received in Holy Baptism."

Only God, for Jesus' sake, can liberate us from the injurious behaviors that take control over us. St. Paul pointed us in the right direction when he cried out, "What a wretched man I am! Who will rescue me from this body of death? Thanks be to God—through Jesus Christ our Lord!" (Romans 7:24). Rescue is through Jesus Christ our Lord and only through Him.

David certainly serves as an example for us. His adulterous and murderous behavior came to oppress him severely. He felt God's hand heavy upon him. He felt his bones wasting away and groaned all day long. Like St. Paul, he was a wretched man. But, in the midst of his acute pain, he remembered and believed that God could and would help him. He wrote, "Blessed is he whose transgressions are forgiven, whose sins are covered. Blessed is the man whose sin the LORD does not count against him" (Psalm 32:1–2).

Jesus assures us that what David believed is what we, too, are to believe. As the Son who sets us free, Jesus forgives our sins and gives us the liberating power of the Holy Spirit. We are to believe this with our whole hearts: "If we confess our sins, He [God] is faithful and just and will forgive our sins and purify us from all unrighteousness" (1 John 1:9).

St. Paul writes at length in his Letter to the Romans about the new life of freedom from sin that God gives us in Baptism. He teaches:

> Don't you know that all of us who were baptized into Christ Jesus were baptized into His death? We were therefore buried with Him through baptism into death in order that, just as Christ was raised from the dead through the glory of the Father, we too may live a new life. If we have been united with Him like this in His death, we will certainly also be united with Him in His resurrection. (Romans 6:3–5).

God can and does forgive our sins for Jesus' sake. In the midst of our struggle against sin, He renews our lives through the work of the Holy Spirit, whom we received in Holy Baptism. He justifies us by declaring us righteous in His sight. He also sanctifies us by renewing our lives through the working of the Holy Spirit. As St. Paul goes on to say, "Count yourselves dead to sin but alive to God in Christ Jesus. Therefore do not let sin reign in your mortal body so that you obey its evil desires" (Romans 6:11–12). In the midst of your powerlessness, believe this. Trust in the promises of God. God is faithful.

Truth 3: Decision for Action

The third truth bids us to "live each day under the Holy Spirit's power so that, in the promise and new life of Holy Baptism, we decisively turn our will and our lives over to the care of God and His re-creating power and make fuller use of His gift of the Holy Spirit to obtain liberation from our controlling sinful behaviors of mind and body."

The critical time for action has come. We begin with our minds because, as we have discussed, our minds generate our feelings and actions. Minds filled with negative thoughts and wrong beliefs give rise to harmful feelings and actions. Thus, under the leading and power of the Holy Spirit, we make a decision in our minds to turn our will and our lives over to the care of God and His re-creating power. We are talking the language of repentance—of having the new mind that turns from sin, embraces God's forgiveness, and receives new power and opportunities from God. St. Paul discussed this subject with the Ephesian Christians:

> You were taught, with regard to your former way of life, to put off your old self, which is being corrupted by its deceitful desires; to be made new in the attitude of your minds; and to put on the new self, created to be like God in true righteousness and holiness. (Ephesians 4:22–24)

Other words of St. Paul that are especially relevant to the third truth are his words in Roman 12. There St. Paul writes: "Do not conform any longer to the pattern of this world, but be transformed by the renewing of your mind. Then you will be able to test and approve what God's will is—His good, pleasing and perfect will" (Romans 12:2).

God Himself renews our minds as His Holy Spirit, given to us in Holy Baptism, works in us through His Word of love. He re-creates us as we live under His Word just as Jesus instructed. "To the Jews who had believed Him, Jesus said, 'If you hold to My teaching, you are really My disciples. Then you will know the truth, and the truth will set you free' " (John 8:31–32). What can we expect as God gives us new minds? We expect and receive the fruit of the Spirit that generate good actions. This fruit, according to St. Paul, is "love, joy, peace, patience, kindness, goodness, faithfulness, gentleness and self-control" (Galatians 5:22–23). Such newness, of course, is never perfect in this life, only in the life of the world to come. But God, who raises the dead, can and does make powerful changes in the lives of sinful people. Thanks to Him, people can be, and are, set free from hurtful behaviors. They are people addicted to a variety of hurtful behaviors and substances. This newness of life, characterized by Christian growth, begins with God's gift of repentance. By His grace, He gives people a new mind.

With the assurance of God's pardon, care, and life-changing power, we decide to "make fuller use of His gift of the Holy Spirit to obtain liberation from controlling sinful behaviors of mind and body." We decide not to receive the grace of God in vain (2 Corinthians 6:1) but to live by the Spirit (Galatians 5:16). We know that God enables us to will and do of His good pleasure (Philippians 2:13). Therefore we determine to make every effort to put into practice the kind of life the Holy Spirit inspires and enables. We determine to make purposeful and energetic use of the power the Holy Spirit supplies. As St. Paul directs us, we will use the Spirit at work in us actively, energetically, and with commitment of purpose to reject hurtful behaviors and rightly to care for ourselves and to love others as we love ourselves. Here are his words:

> Count yourselves dead to sin but alive to God in Christ Jesus. Therefore do not let sin reign in your mortal body so that you obey its evil desires. Do not offer the parts of your body to sin, as instruments of wickedness, but rather offer yourselves to God, as those who

have been brought from death to life; and offer the parts of your body to Him as instruments of righteousness. For sin shall not be your master, because you are not under law, but under grace. (Romans 6:11–14)

Decision in Step 3 assumes and requires doing. What we make a decision to do, we are to do. We are to act on our decision immediately and day by day. Therefore, identify what aspect or aspects of your life you want God to change and put into practice what you have determined to do. Surrendering yourself to God, ask Him to do for you what you cannot do for yourself. By the Spirit's power at work in you, turn your will and life over to the care of God and His life-transforming power. Begin now and each day to use God's gift of the Holy Spirit to change aspects of your thinking, feeling, and acting that need changing.

By the power of God you can experience freedom from hurtful behaviors. You may have setbacks from time to time, but continue to practice Truths 1, 2, and 3 day after day. At times you will no doubt find yourself doing what you do not want to do, as well as what you want to do. But you will increasingly find and possess the freedom Jesus promises. As you practice these steps of daily repentance, with God's help a new person can come forth living in the freedom for which Christ has set you free. This is the way to deal with wrong beliefs, thoughts, attitudes, and their painful emotions and hurtful actions. This is the way to find freedom from jealousy, low self-esteem, worry, fear, sexual immorality, gambling, overspending, the abuse of alcohol, drugs, food, work, power, and relationships, and all hurtful mental and physical behaviors.

5

Liberating Truths 4–9
Dealing with Hurtful Behaviors

Truth 4: Inventory Preparation

Truth 4 introduces actions, supported by Holy Scripture and enabled by God, by which we can perpetuate, reinforce, and enhance our freedom from those behaviors of mind and body for which we are receiving liberation. Truths 4–12 provide a way to live out the gift of daily repentance that God has given us in Holy Baptism. God Himself instructs us on how to deal with the wrongs we have done in a righteous manner as we receive more of His comfort and power, do good to others, and regain a sense of integrity.

We begin by making "a searching and fearless inventory of our besetting sinful and hurtful behaviors of mind and body that require immediate attention." This means we are to be even more thorough than we have been in Step 3 in identifying the specific thoughts, feelings, and actions by which we have sinned against God and damaged ourselves and others. This thoroughness in looking at our sinful behaviors of body and mind will aid us in the expansion of our freedom in living obediently before God and beneficially for ourselves and others.

Scripture encourages us to examine ourselves. "Let us examine our ways and test them, and let us return to the

LORD" (Lamentations 3:40). The psalmist speaks of making a personal inventory: "I have considered my ways and have turned my steps to Your statutes" (Psalm 119:59).

We are to be searching and fearless in making our inventory. We find our strength to do this difficult task in the realization that God already knows all our sins and still loves and accepts us for Jesus' sake. We confess with the psalmist, "O LORD, You have searched me and You know me" (Psalm 139:1). This is the God "who forgives all your sins," says the psalmist (Psalm 103:3).

The making of an inventory indicates the importance of thoughtful introspection and thorough self-examination. It also suggests the preparation of a written list detailing our discoveries. Put your findings into writing. But as you do, remember the wisdom of Luther, who said we should not make confession a torment. For who can know all of his own sins?

Where shall we begin? We begin by focusing on the besetting behavior that we are giving our immediate attention. Then we take a hard look at sinful behaviors associated with our targeted entangling behavior. If our targeted behavior is a behavior of thought, we examine resulting sinful feelings and actions. If we are focusing on a particular feeling, we look at the hurtful thoughts or misbeliefs creating the painful feelings and possible wrong actions. If we are giving attention to a sinful action, we take a hard look at the thoughts and feelings behind the action.

Tyler was looking for lasting freedom from his painful feeling of depression and the associated thoughts and actions. He discovered that entwined with his depression were a number of other behaviors of both mind and body. He had a great deal of anger. He experienced fatigue and difficulty sleeping and had lost his appetite. In turn, he was distant from his family members and friends and was often quite disagreeable. He missed quite a few days at work.

What was generating Tyler's hurtful feelings and painful behaviors? The answer was found in his depression-creating thoughts. Over and over he said to himself, "I'm a worthless person"; "I can't do anything right"; "Nobody cares about me"; "I really have no future"; "God doesn't care about me."

In making his inventory, Tyler listed besetting behaviors connected with his depression that both generated and intensified his depression. He listed anger, sadness, self-depreciating and hopeless thoughts, lack of trust in God, a self-centered lack of care and concern for his family and friends, neglect of his body, impatience, and bad temper.

Joan decided to use the liberating truths to focus on her obsessive thoughts. She thought that her associates at work were undermining her work and trying to get her fired. At times she realized these thoughts were not rooted in fact, and she wanted to rid herself of inappropriate thoughts and the uncomfortable feelings and actions stemming from her negative beliefs.

Joan's thoughts caused her painful feelings. She was filled with suspicion, fear, sadness, anger, resentment, and jealousy. Her actions involved distancing herself from her associates, speaking badly of them when she had occasion, trying to get even with them when she thought they were hurting her. When she made her inventory list, Joan specified all of these hurtful feelings and actions generated by her suspicious thoughts. They needed to be dealt with if she would continue to recover from her paranoia and replace it with positive thoughts that produce good feelings and actions.

Jerry was trying to deal with his alcoholic drinking. He had lost control and wanted to quit drinking. With the doing of Step 3, he did stop drinking, but he knew he must now deal with those thoughts and feelings that had been associated with his drinking. He knew they were a threat to his abstinence and new lifestyle.

Certain thoughts endangered Jerry: "I can't get along without drinking"; "I feel good about myself only when I'm drunk"; "I'm not a real man unless I can drink a lot"; "My only friends are my drinking buddies"; "Only by drinking can I escape my problems"; "I can be sociable only when I'm drinking"; "People don't like someone who doesn't drink"; "Drinking is the only thing that takes away the guilt and fears I feel about my drinking behavior."

Jerry had many harmful feelings to overcome. Among them were feelings of fear, guilt, worthlessness, resentment, and worry. Hurtful actions that accompanied Jerry's drinking behavior included his attempts to control other people's lives, dishonesty, poor work performance, immoral acts, emotional and physical abuse at home, and misuse of money.

In making his written inventory list, Jerry noted the many entangling behaviors linked with his drinking. He listed the wrong thoughts, beliefs, perceptions, and body behaviors identified above. God enabled him to be searching and fearless.

Inventory lists done in compliance with Truth 4 prepare us for the next step, which instructs us how to use our inventory. Being searching and fearless in examining ourselves will pay big dividends.

Truth 5: Admission of Hurtful Behaviors

The fifth truth instructs us to "acknowledge to ourselves and confess to God and another Christian the exact nature of our sinful and hurtful behaviors. Mindful of the comforting and reassuring benefits of individual absolution, we value the opportunity to make private confession before the pastor and receive individual absolution from God through him as God's representative."

The time has come to make use of the inventory of our besetting sinful and hurtful behaviors. First, putting aside our denial, we explore and acknowledge to ourselves how our wrong behaviors of mind and body have very specifically expressed themselves in hurting ourselves and particular people. Tyler, for example, discovered that his depression and attendant behaviors had caused him to lose respect for himself, to stop praying, to neglect his participation in the worship and fellowship of the Christian congregation, to experience physical health problems, and to neglect his appearance. With regard to others, he had become non-communicative and disagreeable with his family and friends. He had done poor work at his place of employment and often used bad language when dealing with his fellow workers. Tyler's list grew longer as he became more specific in identifying the effects of his depression.

Second, we confess to God the exact nature of our sinful behaviors. We follow the example of David, who said to God, "Then I acknowledged my sin to You and did not cover up my iniquity. I said, 'I will confess my transgressions to the LORD'—and You forgave the guilt of my sin" (Psalm 32:5). We act according to the advice and promises of St. John, "If we claim to be without sin, we deceive ourselves and the truth is not in us. If we confess our sins, He is

41

faithful and just and will forgive us our sins and purify us from all unrighteousness" (1 John 1:8–9). We confess our sins to God, and He forgives us our sins for the sake of Jesus' saving life and death. "He who conceals his sins does not prosper, but whoever confesses and renounces them finds mercy" (Proverbs 28:13).

Third, we confess our sins to another Christian. St. James encourages this kind of confession. He writes to Christians, "Confess your sins to each other" (James 5:16). This kind of confession is of great value because it requires and produces humility and honesty and demonstrates genuine repentance. It signifies that we know the seriousness of our wrongdoings and take responsibility for them. Our confession means that we earnestly yearn to walk in newness of life. In turn, our confession leads to assurance of God's love and pardon, His acceptance and empowerment. The Christian before whom we confess assures us that God takes away our sins for Jesus' sake and restores us to live and serve with integrity in the Christian community. Our sins and guilt cause us to withdraw from others into loneliness. They drive us into hiding and separation from others. But our confession and God's Gospel lead back into a fuller experience of the Christian fellowship; we are no longer alone.

The fellow Christian before whom we make our confession may indeed be the pastor. Or we may chose to make our confession before the pastor in addition to confessing before a fellow layperson. In a very special way, God has given pastors the ministry of hearing confessions and pronouncing absolution on His behalf. After His resurrection, Jesus said to His disciples:

> "Peace be with you! As the Father has sent Me, I am sending you." And with that He breathed on them and

said, "Receive the Holy Spirit. If you forgive anyone his sins, they are forgiven; if you do not forgive them, they are not forgiven." (John 20:21–23)

Individual confession and absolution is certainly not required for receiving the forgiveness of sins through faith in Jesus and His death for our sins. But individual confession and absolution, centered in the Gospel of sins forgiven in the blood of Jesus, is a great opportunity that God gives for comfort, reassurance, and restoration. We confess before the pastor for the sake of the absolution and all its comfort and power. We recognize that the voice of the pastor is in actuality the voice of God. When the pastor declares, "I forgive you all your sins in the name of the Father and of the Son and of the Holy Spirit," it is God Himself who says, "I forgive you."

We firmly know and believe that our sins are forgiven before God in heaven. "Mindful of the comforting and reassuring benefits of individual absolution, we value the opportunity to make private confession before the pastor and receive individual absolution from God through him as God's representative."

Confess, and know that the pastor will never reveal what you have said. Be absolved and be relieved in your conscience. Be absolved and be freed from your sins and their oppressive guilt and tyranny in your life.

Truth 6: Readiness for Removal of Hurtful Behaviors

The next truth encourages us to "be ready and willing to have God remove our sinful and hurtful behaviors of mind and body."

Confession and absolution outfit us to amend our lives. Confession and absolution offer us the motivation and empowerment to rid ourselves of our sinful and hurtful behaviors of mind and body. However, it is not easy for us to carry out Truth 6. A part of us is ready and willing. A part of us desires most sincerely and earnestly to have God remove our sins.

Yet, another part of us is reluctant to give up hurtful behaviors that have become so much a part of our lives and may have seemed for a while to meet some need deep within us. We so easily forget the seriousness of our sin and the terrible pain that our behaviors have caused us and others. Thus, we sometimes find it difficult to be "ready and willing." Jesus spoke of this struggle this way: "The spirit is willing, but the body is weak" (Matthew 26:41).

On our part, we need both to realize what is going on within us and to purposefully and vigorously use the outfitting and empowerment of confession and absolution to be ready and willing to have God remove our sinful behaviors. Remember again the words of St. Paul, "It is God who works in you to will and to act according to His good purpose" (Philippians 2:13). With the strength that God gives us we become "ready and willing to have God remove our sinful and hurtful behaviors of mind and body." In the words of St. Paul, "Christ's love compels us, because we are convinced that one died for all, and therefore all died. And He died for all, that those who live should no longer live for themselves but for Him who died for them and was raised again" (2 Corinthians 5:14–15). With the psalmist we pray, "Restore to me the joy of Your salvation and grant me a willing spirit, to sustain me" (Psalm 51:12).

Truth 7: Request for Removal of Hurtful Behaviors

When we are ready and willing to have God remove our sin and hurtful behaviors, we are to act and "ask God, with a humble mind, to remove our sinful and hurtful thoughts, emotions, and actions." Of course we can never achieve complete holiness in this life. But God's grace has a powerful effect on our behavior. With God's help, many have been set free from alcoholism, drug abuse, and other hurtful behaviors.

With humbleness of mind, we pray to God for His aid and assistance. With complete dependence on God, we ask Him to take away the sinful and hurtful behaviors that have been plaguing us and to replace them with Christian behaviors. We pray as did David, "Create in me a pure heart, O God" (Psalm 51:10).

Tyler asked God to take away inaccurate thoughts and beliefs and to remove his anger, sadness, self-depreciating and hopeless thoughts, lack of trust in God, a self-centered lack of care and concern for his family and friends, neglect of his body, impatience, and bad temper. Joan asked God to remove her paranoid thinking, suspicion, fear, sadness, anger, resentment, jealousy, and vengeful actions. Jerry prayed to God to take away his wrong thoughts, his painful feelings of fear, guilt, worthlessness, resentment, and worry. He implored God to rid him of his dishonesty, poor work performance, immoral activities, emotional and physical abusiveness at home, misuse of money, and his need to control other people's behavior.

To "ask God, with a humble mind, to remove our sinful and hurtful thoughts, emotions, and actions" implies that we intend to actively and purposively use God's gift of the

Holy Spirit to rid ourselves of sinful and damaging thoughts, feelings, and activities. We commit ourselves to that for which we pray. We do not sit passively waiting for God to force our sins out of our lives and to compel us to good behavior. We use the power of the Holy Spirit for the purposes that power has been given to us. We use it to work with God in the removal of our sinful and hurtful ways of thinking, feelings, and acting. Recall again these words of St. Paul:

> You were taught, with regard to your former way of life, to *put off* your old self, which is being corrupted by its deceitful desires; to be made new in the attitude of your minds; and to *put on* the new self, created to be like God in true righteousness and holiness. (Ephesians 4:22–24, emphasis added)

In another place Paul exhorts, "Since we live by the Spirit, *let us keep in step with the Spirit*" (Galatians 5:25, emphasis added).

Truth 8: Preparation for Making Amends

The eighth truth suggests that we "make a list of all persons we have harmed and be willing to make amends to each of them." Actually, Truth 4 has prepared us for the doing of Step 8 in much the same way it prepared us to do Step 5. With our searching and fearless inventory before us, we are ready to identify those we have harmed by our sinful and hurtful behaviors of mind and body and exactly how we have hurt them.

On the basis of our inventory, we take pen in hand to make an amends list. This step, too, calls for us to be searching and fearless. It can be frightening and painful for us to consider whom we have hurt, how we have hurt them, and how badly we have hurt them. There can be quite a number of people to consider. Among them are husbands or wives, children, friends, neighbors, employers, colleagues, and fellow church members.

But there is more to carrying out this truth than making a list. This step calls for willingness. It calls us to be willing to make amends to each of them. This willingness, in turn, comes when we recall God's great love for us—that He "sent His one and only Son into the world that we might live through Him. This is love: not that we loved God, but that He loved us and sent His Son as an atoning sacrifice for our sins" (1 John 4:9–10). God's love makes us willing to make amends. As John says, "We love because He [God] first loved us. . . . And He has given us this command: Whoever loves God must also love his brother" (1 John 4:19, 21). We come to agree with the writer of the Proverbs that "fools mock at making amends for sin, but goodwill is found among the upright" (Proverbs 14:9).

Truth 9: Making of Amends

The ninth truth follows closely on the heels of the eighth. Having made a list of all persons we have harmed and having become willing to make amends to each of them, we "make direct amends to the people we have hurt when it is possible to do so without hurting them or others."

Zacchaeus, a chief tax collector, is a New Testament example of a follower of Jesus who made amends. When salvation came to his house, he said, "Here and now I give half of my possessions to the poor, and if I have cheated anybody out of anything, I will pay back four times the amount" (Luke 19:8).

The making of amends is not in any way the grounds for our right relationship with God. Only Jesus and His saving work put us right with God. But, if making amends to particular persons seems wise and desirable, our faith relationship with God and the new life He creates in us give us the desire and the strength to do it. This is the way it was in Zacchaeus's life.

Making amends is not an easy undertaking even when we want to do so. There are obstacles. They are the difficulty of forgiving others, the fear and pride involved in facing others with the admission of wrongs, and purposeful forgetting.

God does not prescribe particular acts of amendment, but He does enable the amendment of life that produces acts of amendment when they seem right to us and as they seem right to us. Such acts of amendment certainly have great value. They heal relationships between alienated people and restore our sense of Christian integrity. Making amends to people we have harmed shows that we are sincere about living the Christian life, and it underscores the reality of God's life-changing power at work in us. The ability and the opportunities to make amends are gracious gifts of God for our well-being and the well-being of others.

This truth includes a word of caution. We are to "make direct amends to the people we have hurt when it is possible to do so without hurting them or others." On the one hand, we are not to spare ourselves in making amends. But, on the other hand, we are not to seek to make amends if such amend-making will hurt the person we have injured or others. We are not to be selfish or thoughtless of others to advance our own interests.

We recall once again the words of the Book of Proverbs:

"Fools mock at making amends for sin, but goodwill is found among the upright" (Proverbs 14:9). We thank God for making it possible for us to make amends. From such actions come many good benefits.

6

Liberating Truths 10–12
Growing and Sharing

Truth 10: Looking to God for Daily Help

Truths 10–12 have to do with growth in Christian living and sharing with others. We need to continue on the road we have begun to travel. We are to grow. We cannot stand still. If we do not grow, we fall backwards in living our new life of freedom. In turn, it is important for our progress and the well-being of others to share what is liberating us from hurtful behaviors.

Truth 10 bids us to look to God for daily help to grow in our freedom and newness of life. It enjoins us to "continue day by day to take a personal inventory and when we sin, promptly acknowledge and confess our sins, ask God's forgiveness for Jesus' sake, and receive God's forgiveness and liberating power to find freedom from disobedient and hurtful behaviors."

We grow in Christian freedom by living the new life we received in Holy Baptism. It is the life of daily repentance that this truth describes. Our Baptism enables us daily to turn from sin and embrace in faith God's love in Christ for the forgiveness of sins and the new life in Christ that is unending.

To live by daily repentance is our greatest need. Sin at work in us and temptations that surround us endanger our life of freedom in Christ. Indeed, sin and temptations would control and overcome us if we had not received "the washing of rebirth and renewal by the Holy Spirit" in Holy Baptism (Titus 3:5) and if we did not faithfully live out the new life given us by practicing daily repentance. As Martin Luther wrote, "It [Baptism] indicates that the Old Adam in us [sin that remains in us] should by daily contrition and repentance be drowned and die with all sins and evil desires, and that a new man should daily emerge and arise to live before God in righteousness and purity forever." As we have already observed, this is the life St. Paul discusses in his Letter to the Ephesians:

> You were taught, with regard to your former way of
> life, to put off your old self, which is being corrupted
> by its deceitful desires; to be made new in the attitude
> of your minds; and to put on the new self, created to
> be like God in true righteousness and holiness. (Ephe-
> sians 4:22–24)

Truth 10 teaches us that we do not apply the liberating truths just once in our lives. Rather, we live in the rhythm of doing over and over again what the truths instruct in whatever order seems necessary. As we do, we grow. We may have our setbacks (and no doubt will), but we go forward in the power of God and increasingly make progress in living our new life of freedom from hurtful behaviors. When we fail, God's love and power keep us from giving up. He keeps us moving onward and upward on the path of Christian living. Like St. Paul we say, "I press on to take hold of that for which Christ Jesus took hold of me" (Philippians 3:12).

This, then, is the way we live: Day by day we take a personal inventory of our successes and failures. When we achieve success, we thank and praise God. When we detect failures in our lives, we "promptly acknowledge and confess our sins, [and] ask God's forgiveness for Jesus' sake." By doing so, we receive God's forgiveness and a new measure of liberating power "to find freedom from disobedient and hurtful behaviors." We look to God for daily help, and we grow in the newness of life.

Truth 11: Using God's Help to Grow

We grow by God's help as we practice daily repentance within the context of Truth 11 using "the Word of God and the Lord's Supper to enhance our faith relationship with God, and through the use of God's Word and prayer obtain a clearer understanding of God's will that the Holy Spirit empowers us to carry out."

The baptismal life of repentance is lived, and only can be lived, under the influence of God at work in us through His Word and the Lord's Supper. God uses His Word of Law and Gospel, of sin and grace, to produce ongoing repentance within us. Through His Word of love and the Supper of our Lord's body and blood He enhances our faith relationship with Him. He assures us of His love, strengthens our faith, and imparts to us a larger portion of the renewing and liberating life of the Spirit.

We live the growth-producing life of repentance as we live under the Word of God and partake of Jesus' body and blood in the sacred Supper for the forgiveness of sins, life, and salvation. The Gospel comes to us in both Word and Meal, and of this Gospel St. Paul writes, "I am not ashamed of the gospel, because it is the power of God for the salvation of everyone who believes" (Romans 1:16).

As we have frequently noted, when God enables us to

have freedom from hurtful behaviors, He replaces hurtful behaviors with good and godly behaviors. As we receive power for life from God through His Word, we also receive instruction about His will, about how we can use His power to live for His glory, our good, and the good of others. He does not let us wonder and wander. He guides and directs us. The psalmist writes, "Your word is a lamp to my feet and a light for my path" (Psalm 119:105). The Scriptures not only make us "wise for salvation through faith in Christ Jesus," but "all Scripture is God-breathed and is useful for teaching, rebuking, correcting and training in righteousness, so that the man of God may be thoroughly equipped for every good work" (2 Timothy 3:15–17).

St. Paul asked God to remove the "thorn" in his flesh. Paul said, "Three times I pleaded with the Lord to take it away from me." But this was not to be. Paul came to discern that the removal of his thorn was not God's will. Paul wrote, "He said to me, 'My grace is sufficient for you, for My power is made perfect in weakness' " (2 Corinthians 12:8–9).

So it is. God's will becomes clearer as we address our prayers to Him and pay careful attention to how He responds in directing our lives, by opening and closing doors. We use "God's Word and prayer to obtain a clearer understanding of God's will that the Holy Spirit empowers us to carry out."

Truth 12: Passing On and Living the Message of Liberation

As Christians we are concerned not only about our personal good but also about the well-being of others. Therefore, Truth 12 reminds us to "pass on the saving and liberating Good News of Jesus Christ to all in need of God's love and power to overcome sinful and hurtful behaviors, and seek to live every facet of our lives in the freedom of God's people."

In enabling us to replace our hurtful behaviors with behaviors beneficial for ourselves and others, God leads us to love others and be of service to them. We rejoice that "the fruit of the Spirit is love, joy, peace, patience, kindness, goodness, faithfulness, gentleness and self-control" (Galatians 5:22–23).

We Christians are called to do good to all people. St. Paul wrote to Titus:

> For the grace of God that brings salvation has appeared to all men. It teaches us to say "No" to ungodliness and worldly passions, and to live self-controlled, upright and godly lives in this present age, while we wait for the blessed hope—the glorious appearing of our great God and Savior, Jesus Christ, who gave Himself for us to redeem us from all wickedness and to purify for Himself a people that are His very own, eager to do what is good. (Titus 2:11–14)

In turn, in his Letter to the Ephesians, Paul said, "We are God's workmanship, created in Christ Jesus to do good works, which God prepared in advance for us to do" (Ephesians 2:10). For the Romans St. Paul had these words: "You have been set free from sin and have become slaves to righteousness" (Romans 6:18).

Our most important good work and our most noble task as Christians in the service of others is to "pass on the saving and liberating Good News of Jesus Christ to all in need of God's love and power to overcome sinful and hurtful behaviors." Jesus mandated us to proclaim the Gospel to everyone everywhere. He called us His witnesses to others.

Jesus came to them [the 11 post-Easter disciples] and said, "All authority in heaven and on earth has been given to Me. Therefore go and make disciples of all nations, baptizing them in the name of the Father and of the Son and of the Holy Spirit, and teaching them to obey everything I have commanded you." (Matthew 28:18–20)

After Easter Jesus said to the 11 disciples, "Go into all the world and preach the good news to all creation. Whoever believes and is baptized will be saved, but whoever does not believe will be condemned" (Mark 16:15–16). Before His ascension Jesus said to His disciples, "You will receive power when the Holy Spirit comes on you; and you will be My witnesses in Jerusalem, and in all Judea and Samaria, and to the ends of the earth" (Acts 1:8).

We share the Good News of Jesus with others by witnessing. This means we tell others about our experience with Jesus. We speak to others about how God has freed us from the guilt, punishment, and control of all our sinfulness and sins through the saving life, death, and resurrection of Jesus Christ. We share with others how God has liberated us from hurtful behaviors of mind and body and renewed our lives. We assure them that they, too, can obtain all the benefits of God's love through faith in Jesus Christ. Through faith, which the Holy Spirit creates by the Gospel, those who need God's love and power to overcome sinful and hurtful behaviors come to possess that love and power.

Our witness benefits us as well as others. As we witness to others, we witness to ourselves. The Gospel we think about and talk about to others strengthens our own faith and new life. All the more, we "seek to live every facet of our lives in the freedom of God's people." And this commitment most certainly demonstrates to others the effectiveness of the Gospel that we share. They are drawn to Jesus by our words of witness and by our example of personal renewal.

7

How to Apply
the Liberating Truths

How are we to apply the liberating truths? As we have already concluded, the use of the 12 liberating truths is not a onetime thing. We are to use them repeatedly throughout our lives as we live by daily repentance. We also know we need to make intentional use of the 12 truths.

So important is the concept of intentionality in using the liberating truths that we need to underscore its significance. Intentionality is essential to the right use of the truths over and over again throughout our lives. It is essential to living the Christian life.

Members of 12-step groups, such as Alcoholics Anonymous, Al-Anon, and Narcotics Anonymous, talk about *working* the steps. The word *working* reminds us that it takes effort to practice the liberating truths we have been discussing. To *work* the truths requires both intentionality and effort.

Often we are inclined to think that doing Christian works and deeds is something God mysteriously compels us to do without effort on our part. We think that if we sit passively and wait, God will intervene in our lives and propel us into action—even when we are resistant. Thus, when we aren't active in thinking right thoughts and doing good deeds, we might find it convenient to excuse ourselves by saying it isn't God's time for us to be up and doing. We might even blame God for our inactivity.

But living a Christian life of freedom and renewal doesn't work automatically whenever and wherever it is supposed to happen. To be sure, it can happen only because God empowers us to Christian action by the life-changing gift of His Holy Spirit who enters our lives when we obtain the forgiveness of sins through faith in Jesus Christ. However, God expects us to employ His enabling power to use His truths to rid ourselves of hurtful behaviors of mind and body and to use our minds and bodies to do what is good and right in the sight of God. "Let your light shine before men, that they may see your good deeds and praise your Father in heaven" (Matthew 5:16). Christ commands us to do good works, and with the command He supplies the grace to obey.

St. Paul teaches us about working with God in living the Christian life. In his letters he makes clear that we do not and cannot cooperate in any way in coming to faith and obtaining forgiveness before God through faith: "No one can say, 'Jesus is Lord,' except by the Holy Spirit" (1 Corinthians 12:3). As Dr. Luther says in the explanation of the Third Article of the Apostles' Creed: "I believe that I cannot by my own reason or strength believe in Jesus Christ, my Lord, or come to Him."

However, in his Letter to the Romans St. Paul teaches us that as baptized people we have been set free from sin and become slaves of righteousness. We were united with Christ's death and resurrection in Baptism in such a way that we died to sin and were raised to live a new life. With a view to our new life in Christ, he exhorts us to make use of our new life. He instructs us, as people alive to God in Christ, to offer ourselves to God, to offer the parts of our body to God as instruments of righteousness, and to offer the parts of our body in slavery to righteousness, leading to holiness (Romans, chapters 6–8). Hear the words St. Paul addressed to baptized people:

Count yourselves dead to sin but alive to God in Christ Jesus. Therefore do not let sin reign in your mortal body so that you obey its evil desires. Do not offer the parts of your body to sin, as instruments of wickedness, but rather *offer yourselves to God,* as those who have been brought from death to life; and *offer the parts of your body to Him as instruments of righteousness.* For sin shall not be your master, because you are not under law, but under grace. (Romans 6:11–14, emphasis added)

St. Paul offers similar advice in other Letters in the New Testament.

Galatians 5:16: "So I say, live by the Spirit."

Galatians 5:25: "Since we live by the Spirit, let us keep in step with the Spirit."

Ephesians 4:22–24: "You were taught, with regard to your former way of life, to put off your old self, which is being corrupted by its deceitful desires; to be made new in the attitude of your minds; and to put on the new self, created to be like God in true righteousness and holiness."

Ephesians 5:8–10: "You were once darkness, but now you are light in the Lord. Live as children of light (for the fruit of the light consists in all goodness, righteousness and truth) and find out what pleases the Lord."

Colossians 3:10: "Put on the new self, which is being renewed in knowledge in the image of its Creator."

Then, there is St. Paul's splendid paragraph in Romans 12:1–2:

Therefore, I urge you, brothers, in view of God's mercy, to offer your bodies as living sacrifices, holy and pleasing to God—this is your spiritual act of worship. Do not conform any longer to the pattern of this world, but be transformed by the renewing of your mind. Then you will be able to test and approve what God's will is—His good, pleasing and perfect will.

St. Paul's key words to indicate deliberate, intentional, and vigorous use of God's power for change are "offer yourselves," "live by the Spirit," "keep in step with the Spirit," "live as children of light," "put on the new self," and "offer your bodies." He most certainly teaches intentional and energetic use of God's life in us to grow in Christian living. This is the way we apply the truths of liberation from hurtful behaviors. This is the way we grow daily, day after day, in freedom from hurtful behaviors and in producing the fruit of the Spirit. This is our way of living the abundant life of repentance.

Conclusion

Many people suffer from tenacious hurtful behaviors of mind and body. Disobedient to God, these behaviors dishonor God and hurt us and others. But, thanks be to God, all of us who yearn for freedom from hurtful behaviors have hope and help available to us. We have hope and help for freedom from our persistent behaviors that are like thieves that steal, kill, and destroy. We have hope and help for joyful and productive lives.

Our hope and help come from God, who sent His Son to our world to make good for our sins. He did this by living a life of perfect obedience to God, by suffering death on the cross as the payment for our sins before a holy God who must punish sin, and by rising from the dead triumphant over sin, death, and all that is evil.

Freedom from sinful and hurtful behaviors of body and mind become ours as God's gift as, through the announcement of His love in Christ, He gives us faith to believe in Jesus Christ as Savior and to trust Him for the freedom we need. Through faith in Jesus, God forgives our sinfulness and sin, the guilt of our sin, and the condemnation due us because of our disobedience. In Christ, God declares us right and righteous before Himself, claims us as His own, and makes us new persons by the work of the Holy Spirit. God sets us on the road of obtaining freedom from hurtful behaviors and living the new life in Christ.

The truths we have been discussing outline the way of

liberated living that God provides and sets before us in the Bible. In the power of the Holy Spirit, apply these truths. Find freedom from hurtful behaviors. Find genuine freedom in service to God and others. We will not become perfect persons because sin remains in us as long as we live this side of heaven. We will have relapses and setbacks in living the Christian life throughout our lives. But we will experience victories in the direction of freedom that we never imagined. Making robust and intentional use of the Spirit's power to live according to the truths God provides, we will make progress in the realm of liberation and newness of life. We will know the joy of God's salvation.

Keep on claiming the promise of Jesus that we have affirmed throughout this book: "If you hold to My teaching, you are really My disciples. Then you will know the truth, and the truth will set you free" (John 8:31–32). "If the Son sets you free, you will be free indeed" (verse 36).

You are free indeed! Live out your freedom. Live out your freedom and newness of life. God will give you His rich blessings.